HOW TO MAKE MONEY FROM HOME

7 STEPS TO EARN MONEY FROM BAKING RECIPES

CHARLOTTE MOYER

Receive my next book for free!
Exclusive promotions, updates and newsletters
Join my Book Club Now

TABLE OF CONTENTS

WELCOME

Firstly I'd like to thank you and congratulate you for downloading "How to Make Money from Home: 7 Steps to Earn Money from Baking Recipes".

Inside this book are some pearls of wisdom that I know you will find helpful and easy to put into action. It's time to take advantage of these amazing steps and take the leap of starting your own venture.

Let's get started!

Thank you

Charlotte Moyer

PS...Don't forget to join my Book Club

INTRODUCTION

Baking. The process of getting some flour, some sugar, a few eggs, salt, oil, water, milk and a myriad of other base materials, pouring them in a mixer, a few oven forms and creating masterpieces of taste and enjoyment for everyone. Cookies, bread, cupcakes, cakes, pies you name it. We all love them and we are all looking forward to the next time our mother, wife, sister, father, brother or whoever else makes some more.

It is well-known why we all prefer home baked goods. First of all we are sure what they are made of. Genuine, one hundred percent natural ingredients without any added chemical preservatives and additives to lengthen their shelf life time or to make them maintain their shape, texture and form for the time it takes to get sold to the general public, which may even reach to as long as a few months.

It is the same combination of ingredients that guarantees the huge difference in taste between home-baked goods and commercially available products. There is nothing comparable to the taste and aroma of a freshly baked cookie as it comes right out of the oven. It may burn at first as it is still hot but this is a rather small price to pay for the pleasure.

Discovering and developing a joy for baking presents an opportunity to earn some extra income from doing something you love. All the above being said, it becomes a real question whether this could be a hobby that could provide enough income to supplement or provide a full time salary. The answer is, yes!

A baking business from home or a full-fledged bakery can grow to flourish into as successfully profitable business. In order to achieve maximum success there are some essential steps that need to be taken. This book will guide you through these basic foundations in 7 easy steps and will set you on your way to getting started.

Baking for a few hundred people is be quite a daunting thought. Not only does it require a much greater preparation time (a person can only knead that much dough over the course of a day), but it also requires greater equipment, more ingredients and a distribution network to get the baked stuff to the people who want it. The electric bills will be greater, the money to buy the ingredients will be more and in the end how much is someone's time and effort really worth?

It needs careful planning and proper marketing to make it so that prices are competitive. Customers will be willing to pay a little more for the pleasure of homemade baked goods if they are great quality, delicious and are marketed well. However the general problem is that not everyone who wants to get into such an endeavor has adequate knowledge of product quality, pricing, planning or marketing to make themselves competitive.

Then, it is necessary to make sure that the relevant legislation allows you to sell your own home made baked goods. You may have to abide by safety regulations, certain taxation prerequisites, checking that you abide by any laws in place that may forbid a person to sell directly to the general public without the intervention of a certified food distribution agent.

There are a lot of opportunities and challenges involved in a decision to start your own business. All of which will need to be considered and weighed carefully if the venture is to result in a successful and profitable livelihood.

Now that we've got you thinking, it's time to get started!

THE NOTION OF BAKING

The idea of making money out of baking is as old as the formation of coherent sovereign states that went further than the process of bartering for their economies. The sale of bread is the first recorded such venture. Initially in inns, taverns and hotels, then in bakeries and other similar establishments. Then came pies, cakes, jams and everything else. A good baker was actually a very well respected member of society.

As long as it was kept local and the ingredients used were pure and natural there was no problem. Each baker had their own recipes which built their name, each area was famous for a certain kind of pie, a different kind of cake or a set of chocolate products. However, the steady increase of the population required industrialization of the baking processes which led to the inclusion of ingredients that altered everything.

Time and again, there would be someone who thought that they could produce better baked products and went into the market with the recipes and the ingredients that they thought would make the difference. Some of them remained in business for a very short time. Some others lasted a little longer. A few became legendary and in the end became industrialized and entered the same world they wanted to resist.

There are many reasons for wanting to go into the baking industry. Most will decide to try it in an attempt to expand their hobby while others do so to solve their financial circumstance. There have been many documented cases of women that saved their families from impoverishment and added to the income of the family enough to stay afloat.

There have also been documented cases where people did it because they had plenty of time in their hands and had nothing else to do with it. In their case it wasn't for the money at all. It was for having something to occupy themselves with. If out of it came a decent income, this was a welcome byproduct and not the original objective.

Some others were actually compelled into baking by their husbands or families. Especially in cases where the recipe was so successful that people were lining up to taste every new batch. In these cases it wasn't the bakers themselves that needed or wanted the money that came out of the enterprise. It was the other people around them that wanted to take advantage of their abilities.

It really doesn't matter what the reason behind the choice to make an income out of baking is. What matters is that after the decision is taken, the correct steps are taken so that the attempt does not end in failure.

Psychologically speaking, no one should get involved with a venture if their hearts are not into it. If you want to get into it out of your own initiative, which is a much more preferable arrangement, then reading the next chapter will make sure that your heart's desire will also be escorted by your pocket's desire to get full.

STEP 1: THE LEGALITIES

To make an income out of baking actually prohibits you from gambling on what to do. There are steps, procedures and actions to be taken that have been time and again tested for their successful outcomes. You may resent some of them and you may consider that some others may hinder your productivity. However, you are getting into this to be successful and make a profitable income so you need to make sure that you will make money.

In fact, the first steps must be taken before you make your final decision. These steps have to do with the legal coverage of the venture. Imagine what would happen of you decided to bake your first batch only to find out that the laws of your area do not allow you to sell them. Wouldn't that be a waste of time and money?

Therefore, before you spent the first cent into purchasing ingredients, you need to go to a legal library, search the internet, or seek professional advice on the subject. Some jurisdictions require that there can be no direct sale to the general public without the intervention of an already licensed enterprise. However, this is a very rare circumstance and can be circumvented.

There is no legislation worldwide that does not require a license for the slightest sale of any kind of food. This means that you need to become aware of all the details and the paperwork required. It usually means that someone from the health department will come and inspect the preparation premises to check if they comply with certain health and safety regulations. It is to ensure that your cleanliness and food safety will be exemplary. But wouldn't it be a shame to lose a license because you may have not purchased a fire extinguisher?

You should also be prepared that this inspection could be repeated several times and that you may be required not to work from your own home environment but through a food production environment, which means that you may have to rent the appropriate space.

Other issues in the relevant legislation may require specific types of packaging which may mean that you must sell all your products in plastic wrappings. This means that you will have to calculate in your initial investment the relevant associated costs. However, there is one issue that you need to consider for your initial investment regardless whether it's required by the relevant legislation or not.

No matter how careful you may be and how perfectly you may prepare everything, accidents do happen as there are always unforeseen circumstances. Any accident could cost you a fortune, even imprisonment, which makes it imperative that you need to be covered with a liability insurance policy. It may not sound ethical and you may become deeply discouraged if anything, God forbid, happened, but it is one of these mandatory things that we talked about in the beginning of the chapter.

Another issue required by law almost everywhere in the world is to include the ingredients in the label of the baked goods. This can be covered very easily with your own home computer and printer. However, when you choose the packaging of your products you will have to make sure that there is ample space for the label at a position that will not damage the baked food.

We assume that you are aware that hard work will be required of you even after the legislation has been dealt with. And it is not just hard work. You may also have to get intuitive, imaginative and more creative than you have never been before. Let's explore these issues in the next chapter.

Step 2: What you will need to pitch in

In the previous chapter we discussed the legalities. Some may have thought that it should have been discussed after addressing first the one most important issue involved. That you do actually know how to bake. The entire context of this book assumes that you do. If you don't there is nothing to discuss about it. There is only one directive here:

Learn how to bake

Actually this is a two prone directive. Presumably you do know how to bake a cake, a pie or a handful of cookies. And it would be a rather natural process to practice your best recipes and study to improve on your baking skills.

However, baking is an art. And you need to develop an appreciation of the art. If you are not into cooking or baking then it is unlikely that you will be successful. The prerequisite is that your baking speaks to you the same way music speaks to a musician, writing speaks to an author, sculpting speaks to a sculptor.

The best thing to do to hone your skills is to try different baking techniques before going in business. A good tactic is to start changing quantities and ingredients and have people taste the new baked goods until you reach the desired results.

Keep in mind that you will not be able to satisfy everyone. Every person's sense of taste is different. Some may like more sugar, others may like more aroma, and others may want more varieties of flavor. What you need to go for, is the greatest possible number of satisfactory comments on the average.

Making money out of baking is a venture gaining momentum especially in places where there is a lot of financial instability. Therefore, the competition will be strong in the industry. There will be others baking the similar cakes, jams, cupcakes and pies as you. It stands to reason that to survive the competition you need to add a few twists to stand out from the crowd.

BAKE UNUSUALLY

Within your skill honing attempts you may also want to try to bake in a way that will surprise your clients. Unusual ingredients, different recipes, unusual shapes and unexpected flavor combinations will do that for you. This is actually where your innovation, imagination and creativity are required.

In this effort you may want to consult recipes from different parts of the world. For example a dish that characterizes Libya and is made nowhere else in the world is liver with raisins. Should we even mention moussaka or haggis? The same stands true for baked cookies, cakes and pies. There are plenty of references online for a myriad of options available.

The best thing is that you do not even have to repeat the same recipe. A good variation will do just as well maybe even better. Want an example? Strudel and apple pie. Basically the same or similar thing but completely different at the same time. The opinions vary on which of the two is better.

BAKE UNIQUELY

Different tastes and shapes is only half of the equation. The other half is uniqueness. Let's throw some ideas on the table:

A package of 26 chocolate chip cookies shaped in the letters of the alphabet.

A package of cookies shaped in currency signs. How many cookies have you seen out there looking like a $? Or a £? Or a €?

Small pies shaped in the signs of the zodiac.

Combine all the above together and now you are thinking outside of the box. Setting your products apart from the rest is what will give you a unique selling point.

Now that you have your juices flowing on wonderful baking ideas. The next step is to consider what to charge. That is to ensure that you do the math and price your products correctly. If you sell a pie for $5 and it costs you $10, it's bad business. If you sell the same pie for $20 you are probably too expensive. Let's discuss the basics of what you need to know about reaching a fair selling price for your baked goods.

STEP 3: SETTING THE PRICES

People that set the prices on the commercially available foods, have studied an entire course at college on this. Many will tell you that all you need to do is evaluate your time and effort, add the cost you paid in ingredients and the preparation process and that's it. In most cases if you follow that rule your prices will be too high.

As aforementioned, people are prepared to pay something extra for fresh home baked products. Something extra does not mean double the price of a similar commercial product. Especially in times of financial crises or in poorer areas. Therefore, you will need to be a little more careful on how to set the prices.

Let's try to keep things simple. In order to get a better price for the ingredients you have to buy large quantities otherwise it's more often than not won't be cost effective. You will need to source are the right cost and ensure that you don't buy too much ingredients. Otherwise you will lose money through waste and have to dispose of some of the ingredients without using them. If you buy too little you will bake less products.

After you have tested your skills a number of times you instinctively know how to calculate the quantities you need. This will help you to calculate the exact cost of these quantities. Using these firm quantities allows you to keep a complete tally on the amount of ingredients you need for all of your variety of products. We strongly suggest that when purchasing your ingredients in bulk that you negotiate discounts at every opportunity.

Of course the other costs associated to bake your goods are bills and equipment usage. You will have to use an oven which will increase the electric bill. It is important that you are familiar with the costs of each bill before and after setting up your venture. Many companies provide breakdowns with each bill on the costs of usage.

If you have to work outside your home, any machinery that you may have had to buy in order to comply with the licensing requirements, the packaging material for the baked goods and all other such expenses also need to be factored into the overall costs.

In the end you add amounts all the costs together and come up with the total that comes out of your pockets every month for being able to remain in business. You need to make sure that it is at least this amount that is collected from your monthly sales in order to breakeven.

You will then need to calculate from the above amount what your profit will be. Not forgetting your tax liabilities that need to be paid.

Based on this, it's not just the time and effort that will give you your income. It's the correct evaluation of the market and the competition you are facing. In this concept it does not really matter how much the commercially available pastry goes for. No one will care unless the difference is outrageous.

It may take a month or two to find out the correct balance between an acceptable income and competitive rates. You should be prepared that at least in the beginning to spend a lot of time researching your competitors and adjusting your products. This is the natural process and you should not be surprised.

Also in the natural process of things are the methods that you will use to attract clients to buy what you sell. And those are explored in the next chapter.

Step 4: Marketing

Ever wondered why professional marketers get the high salaries they do? Because they devise the most successful ways to attract the public's attention to the products they want to sell. In this infinite wisdom of theirs, sometimes they can come up with all the great ways to do their job. However, it is not all difficult. All it takes is some creativity and expanding your knowledge of online marketing strategies.

No one expects you to know everything there is to know about marketing and promotion at the time of starting your venture. However, you will need to get to grips with this quickly if you are to be successful. In Step 1 we explored how to identify your unique selling point and stand out from the crowd.

Nevertheless, people must get to know you. In the beginning this will be achieved with the usual mouth to mouth recommendation. The better your baking is, the faster they will talk about you. However, this will only provide you with a limited customer base.

To increase your customer base you will need to do some promotion. Since you already have (presumably) some knowledge and experience with online platforms such as Facebook or Twitter, these would be a great place to get started. These will cover not only your immediate neighborhood but also your city and beyond.

To get more customers from further away your best option is to set up and run a website site. Not only for information. A full online store will not only get you clients from everywhere around your city, but if your baking is excellent, the orders could be coming in from everywhere and anywhere. At that point the question will be whether you will be able to handle the load of the orders or not. This is a great problem to have!

Another available option is to become mobile. There are plenty of people selling off their goods and produce at local fairs, markets, festivals and other public events. These provide a great opportunity to increase your base locally and the pitch fees are often very low. If this is something you would like to pursue make sure that your license covers such an activity.

Packaging should also be a part of your marketing strategy, the wrappings and the choices you will make for the presentation of your products are very important. They say we eat with our eyes, so for many people the appearance is as important as the taste. How many times have you seen situations where someone would not even approach food if it didn't look right? Also it is not just the appearance of the cake or the pie itself it is also the appearance of the box that you will put it in or the plastic wrap that you will wrap it around.

Always remember that unless you keep your products in an enclosed merchandizer, the law says that they must be wrapped tight to prevent any contamination by external agents.

The secret is to market your products in every way possible that does not include a high cost at first. After your venture has developed, we suggest that you go through other means of marketing, presumably you will have the funds to expand and go on to a more professional means of marketing.

The next important issue to consider is the way that you will sell your products. It is not such as easy as you may think so let's discuss this in the next chapter.

STEP 5: SELLING YOUR PRODUCTS

One of the reasons to actually select to sell your products from a site other than your home is the volume of clients you will be getting on a daily basis. And this is what will happen if you have a natural or acquired aptitude towards baking, once you have developed an innovative and creative set of recipes, your products are sure to earn the reputation of uniqueness.

People will be lining up to order your home baked goods or queuing up in front of the counters that you display your cakes or pies in.

We are in the age of the internet and we have already discussed the usage of a website as a marketing tool. In an era that everyone is just punching keyboards to order everything, the same page must work as a fully serviceable online store. As always the problem with online stores is delivery.

Your baked products must always arrive at their destinations in great quality and on time for any occasion. They cannot arrive stale, damaged or late. They must be completely fresh. The difference in taste and quality will be a dead giveaway.

Customer is king and your customer service must be exceptional. You must cannot forget to offer the upmost satisfaction to each customer no matter the method of their order. In this concept you need to balance between the time you need to prepare the daily product volume and the time that it will take you to prepare the custom orders. Hire extra help if necessary, ask neighbors to help, ask relatives to help but under no circumstances are you to neglect the product quality in your daily volume in order to satisfy a custom order.

Some people question the wisdom of satisfying a custom order. The advantages are many. The best one being that while your everyday production are for a set variety of goods. A custom order is a chance to show your skills and give the customer exactly what they want and specifically for the occasion they want. Whether it be a wedding cake, or cupcakes for a baby shower. This is also a great opportunity to increase income and showcase your work to wider audiences.

Furthermore, a custom order is your chance to come on top of the competition. Imagine the impact to your brand name if you manage to get a custom order for a major event with many attendants. If at the end of the day people are asking how to get in touch with you, it is most probable that you will see an increase of sales.

Selling whatever you bake is, in the final analysis, the process that will earn you the money you need or want. It is the end game that begun with a planning and learning processes. And it is these are things that should be paid the most attention.

However, this is not the end of it yet. We told you that it will take a lot of hard work to accomplish your task. This hard work includes some other little secrets that you should consider to help develop a good and strong brand name. These little secrets are explored in the next chapter.

STEP 6: LITTLE SECRETS

The difference between building a good enterprise and building a great enterprise is the attention to details. So far we discussed the marketing options, price setting, the legal issues and the best way to sell your products. However, this is just the framework and the general concept.

In essence what we have done so far is to lay down the concrete, the brick and the wood construction of a building, we have finished the electrical wires and the plumbing. Now what we discuss will add the doors, the windows and the paint.

CHECK THE ENVIRONMENT

When you need to make money out of an operation you need to know that people are going to buy what you sell. We are talking about baking. Cakes, pies, cookies etc... It would be of no use if you lived in an area with 6 bakeries and three online stores selling the same stuff within a radius of 4 or 5 blocks. Ideally an area with either none or only one bakery at a 20 minute drive distance gives you the first element of the equation for success.

People buy baked products when they do not have the time, the inclination or the talent to bake some themselves. Living in an area full of housewives staying at home, in most likelihood means that they do some baking themselves.

If on the other hand, you live in an area where you see everyone's cars driving out in the morning and coming back late in the afternoon or early in the evening, it is most probable that you already have your clientele set up for you. Even better if we are talking about young couples, newlyweds, people without children or corporate employees.

RECIPES, RECIPES, RECIPES

We repeatedly mentioned that one of the key parts of success is the taste of your products. One of the problems of baking at home is that we do not really pay attention to what we do. We do it mechanically. This is why each time the taste is a little different. This is why sometimes we even produce a batch that is inconsistent or rather unsuccessful (to put it mildly).

This cannot happen if you are going to bake products to make a living. The taste, the texture, the quality, everything must be constant. You cannot sell a batch that "tastes funny" or "tastes like chicken" (to use a known joke).

The best thing to do about it, is after you have performed the initial tests and you have finalized the recipes that you will use, write them down and print them up in a hard copy. Then always pay attention to what you do. Do not let experience take you away and do things mechanically. That will cost you money and probably a lot of it.

That way, if there is any need for you to go away for a while (everyone needs a vacation from time to time) whoever fills in your shoes will have a reference to work with. Just make sure that this person has watched what you do often enough and closely enough so that you can have a level of trust in their skills and capabilities.

EXPAND YOUR OPTIONS

The chapter about selling your products covers the basic aspects of selling over the counter, through deliveries and online. This assumes that the premises that you have rented offer adequate space for you to have a counter and a cash register. It also assumes that you can own and operate an online store.

However, this may not always be the case. Not everyone is adept in the use of the internet (although this is important) and it could be very possible that you could afford only to rent a small space that offers no possibility of housing a counter. This is not a reason to lose hope. There are other options available so that you can increase sales and expand your venture.

For example, if you live in an area for quite some time, it is most probable that you have become friendly with all the shop owners in the area. You can use this to strike deals with let's say the owner of your grocery store, or your local mini market store, to put your baked products on their merchandizers and have the shop owners sell your products for you.

Off course, you would have to offer them a commission for their services which would cut down on your profits, but it is a far better deal than not being able to sell your products at all.

Now that we have put in the doors, the windows and the paint, it is time to put in the furniture. And that will be done by the things to avoid at all costs as discussed in the next chapter.

STEP 7: THINGS NOT TO DO

Even the best professionals cannot avoid mistakes. Mistakes are costly. However, this does not mean that you cannot make every effort to avoid mistakes by taking the necessary precautions. Mistakes can be costly but can be minimized or better still, avoided.

We have already discussed about the consistency of your products, acquiring liability insurance and listing the ingredients as the relevant law requires. These are the most common mistakes made by people who enter into such a venture without any previous knowledge on how to run such an enterprise.

Now it's time to check on a few more.

DO NOT GET SLOPPY WITH THE TAX ISSUES

Crucially at the beginning when it is most possible that you will sell to friends and relatives it is very easy to overlook the tax legislation. Do not. If you are required to issue receipts, do so. For every single item you sell and for every single quantity. If you get inspected and you are found violating the taxation laws that will be the end of it.

However, this is not the only problem with taxes. Some issues may not be violations, but they can result in such damage that you will find yourself owning to your local IRS service a huge amount of money. If you do not promptly record all your expenses you will be subject to a dramatic overhead charge, not to mention getting taxed for an income you never had.

Every invoice and every single cent you pay should be recorded so that it can be exempted. To understand the issue, let's assume that you sell a box of cookies for $10. To collect these $10 you need to pay for the gas for the delivery person to get there, the delivery person's salary and the rest of the expenses that we have already analyzed. The total amount of expenses for these $10 comes up to $8 which means that your actual profit is $2. If out of these $8, $1 goes for gas and you fail to record this receipt, then the IRS will assume that your profit was $3 instead of $2 and tax you accordingly.

Read the taxation requirements carefully. It is strongly recommended that if you have any problems understanding the issues, you should hire an accountant.

DO NOT GET SLOPPY WITH THE DELIVERIES

One of the great differences between the commercially available baked products and the home made ones is the addition of chemicals to make the products more stable and robust. That way they can withstand the hardships of shipping and arrive at their destination in one piece.

Homemade products on the other hand are often more fragile. Which means that you need to find ways to make sure that they do not break up or get damaged in any way as they are transported to their destination. This may require specialized shock absorbing boxes or any other means of making sure that they will get delivered in one piece.

It goes without saying but under no circumstances do you want to disappoint your customers with the quality of the products when they arrive.

DO NOT MISLEAD ON YOUR INGREDIENTS

The law says that you have to list all the ingredients that you use inside your products. No one is asking you to give away your recipes but you cannot hide an ingredient in an attempt to prevent anyone from copying your product. Either hiding or lying about the ingredient list will get you in trouble with the law.

Being ethical on your product ingredients can also been a great selling point for your venture. You must also consider that your goods are made for consumption so customers need to be fully informed on what they are eating beforehand. Some customers may have serious allergies or intolerances to certain ingredients. For example nut allergies, lactose or gluten intolerances etc. Some of these are life threatening, so this is not to be taken lightly.

Getting on to the market to sell baked products is a dream for many people. A dream that they do not dare make true for fear failing in the areas detailed in this book. This is a great misconception. Actually all that is required of you is to make sure that you cover all the bases by doing your research, adequately planning, seek professional assistance where necessary and strategically promoting your goods.

CONCLUSION

Everyone loves pies, cakes, cupcakes and everything else that comes out of baking. In family gatherings they are expected with much anticipation as they are always a source of enjoyment and one of these little moments that make like worth living. People that do not have either the time or the talent or the will to bake these things themselves, always crave for an opportunity to taste some homemade delights.

While commercial baked products are always available and offered at very low prices, everyone knows that they neither taste the same, nor feel the same, nor smell the same as a freshly baked batch that just came out of the home oven.

To combine this with the notion to make a dream come true and sell these freshly baked and homemade products to whomever wants them, is one of the best reasons to get into the business of earn money from your baking passion. Other reasons might be to try and save the family or oneself from financial struggles, to add to the family income or simply because you enjoy it.

No matter what the reason maybe for opening a business to sell baked products to the general public, there are many issues to pay attention to and many tricks of the trade to observe in order to indeed make a profit and not end up losing money.

Remaining within the boundaries of law, taxation and the health safety regulations is the first and foremost consideration.

The idea is to be successful in this business. Even if you have learned to bake, practiced and improved you skills. Find or create unusual and unique recipes, imagine and create unique shapes and think of fashionable and charming ways to package your products. This is the first part of the equation.

The second part is to make sure that the prices you set are both going to provide you with profit and are competitive enough to make it against your competitors. The prices, your marketing choices and the ways that you choose to sell your products are your passport to success.

Paying attention to the little secrets like making sure that your environment will favor your venture and that you can make it work for you, along with the importance of maintaining consistency in the quality of what you produce is the stamp to this passport.

The last issue to consider and the last question to respond to is whether you are ready to acquire this passport and this stamp. And this is something you are capable of knowing. We hope that this book was able to provide you with all the necessary information that you would need to get started. We wish you the very best of luck with your venture.

GOOD LUCK and HAPPY EARNINGS!

ABOUT THE AUTHOR

I am a mother to three beautiful children and a wife to a wonderful husband. I have a passion to teach others and can often be found volunteering in my local community.

During college I worked within my family catering business to support myself. After graduating I opened a chain of small cafes that I ran successfully for a number of years. Now whilst being a stay at home mom, I am able share my skills, knowledge and experience through my books. I feel a great deal of satisfaction when helping others and seeing them flourish to their maximum potential.

Please check out my author page on Amazon to see my latest publications. Please don't forget to **join my Book Club** for a free books, newsletters and updates.

Once again I want to thank you for reading my book. I really hope you got a lot out of it.

If you enjoyed this book I would really appreciate it if you could leave me a positive review on Amazon. You can **click here** to go directly to the book on Amazon and leave your review.

I love getting feedback from my readers and reviews on Amazon really do make a difference. I read all my reviews and would really appreciate your thoughts.

Thanks so much.

CHARLOTTE MOYER

OTHER BOOKS BY AUTHOR

How to Bake Perfectly: 101 Tips, Tricks & Cheats for Baking Recipes – Coming soon!